Sequoyah

History Maker Bios

Laura Hamilton Waxman

BARNES
&NOBLE
BOOKS
NEW YORK

Map on p. 7 and 37 by Laura Westlund
Illustrations by Tim Parlin

Text copyright © 2004 by Lerner Publications Company
Illustrations copyright © 2004 by Lerner Publications Company
2004 Barnes & Noble Books

This 2004 Barnes & Noble Books edition published by
arrangement with Lerner Publications Company,
a division of Lerner Publishing Group, Minneapolis, MN.

ISBN: 0-7607-3917-X

Printed in the United States of America

10 9 8 7 6 5 4 3 2 1

TABLE OF CONTENTS

O nv   le   5 mo   nu   D a   ka

U da   A nu   S ga

hn

su

wi

yv

tsi

dla

di

wa

tle

wo   yo   tlu   ya

s   wu   tla   qua   ha

lo   we   sa   qu

W   T   E   G   C

INTRODUCTION

In 1821, Sequoyah gave the Cherokee people a great gift. He gave them talking leaves. "Talking leaves" was the Cherokee name for writing. For hundreds of years, Sequoyah's people had no way of writing down their own language. Sequoyah changed that with his invention of the Cherokee alphabet.

There are many stories about how Sequoyah invented the Cherokee alphabet. Some are different from others. But the most important facts are the same. Sequoyah invented a way for the Cherokee to write and read in their own language. And he shared his belief with them that they could do anything they set their minds to.

This is his story.

1 CLEVER BOY

Sequoyah was probably born between 1760 and 1770 in the Cherokee village of Tuskegee in present-day Tennessee. The village sat in a peaceful clearing near wooded hills and the cool Tennessee River. Many Cherokee villages lay along both shores of the river.

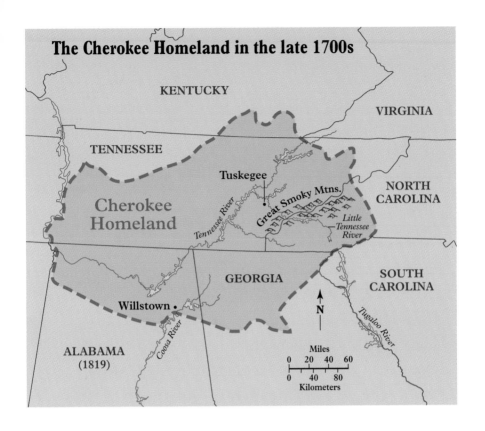

The Cherokee Homeland in the late 1700s

Sometimes Sequoyah went by the name George Guess, which was also spelled "Gist." This name came from his father, a white man whom Sequoyah had never known. Sequoyah was raised by his mother, Wurteh, on a small farm. Wurteh taught her son how to milk the cows, tend the garden, and work the cornfields. Sequoyah was clever, and he learned each new task easily.

Small villages such as Tuskegee and this one were scattered throughout the Cherokee homeland.

But easy tasks were not enough for Sequoyah. He loved to challenge his mind with tough problems. As a young boy, he noticed that the milk from his mother's cows went sour quickly. Sequoyah thought and thought about how to keep the milk fresher longer.

He knew that milk stayed fresh when it stayed cool. He thought of the cool water that flowed in a small creek near his home. It gave him an idea. He decided to build a small wooden cabin right over the creek. Then he stored his mother's milk on the cabin's floor. The water running below kept the milk cool and fresh.

When Sequoyah grew older, Wurteh gave him a new job. He had to watch over her colts. The young horses were frisky and liked to stray far from home. But Sequoyah knew that horses loved salty things. The colts would stick around if they had salt to lick. By watching other Cherokee farmers, he learned to chop down small trees and cut grooves into the logs with a knife. Then he packed the grooves with salt. His mother's colts always came back to the farm to lick the tasty "lick logs" he'd made for them.

Sequoyah learned a clever trick to keep the family's playful colts near home.

In his twenties, Sequoyah thought of a new task for his clever mind. He decided to become a silversmith. Many Cherokee men and women enjoyed wearing silver jewelry. Sequoyah thought he could learn to make the most popular fashions.

THE CHEROKEE HOMELAND

The Cherokee people were once spread out over the southeastern United States. They lived in parts of present-day North and South Carolina, Georgia, Alabama, Virginia, West Virginia, Tennessee, and Kentucky. Long before Sequoyah was born, Europeans began settling in the Cherokee homeland. Over time, Europeans bought parts of the land from Native American leaders. Other times, they stole it. The homeland got smaller and smaller. The Cherokee people wanted to keep peace with their white neighbors. But they did not want to give up any more land.

These Cherokee from the 1700s wear beautiful silver jewelry. Sequoyah learned to make his own jewelry.

Over time, Sequoyah collected silver coins from white settlers living nearby. Then he taught himself how to melt the silver and shape the hot liquid into earrings, chains, and bracelets. Soon he was famous for his beautiful silver creations.

Sequoyah noticed that white jewelers had a special way of marking their names on all the jewelry they made. He did not know how to read or write. The Cherokee language was only spoken. Still, he thought, it would be nice to mark the jewelry he made.

One day, Sequoyah asked a white man to show him how to write the name "George Guess." He practiced and practiced until he could engrave that name on everything he made. It seemed that Sequoyah could do just about anything he set his mind to.

2 TALKING LEAVES

Sequoyah earned a good living as a silversmith. But the work had become too easy for him. Easy work made him bored. Being bored made him lazy. He stopped working so hard.

Sequoyah didn't like the person he had become. He needed a challenge to lift his spirits. He gave up his work as a silversmith. Instead, he plunged into the hard, hot work of being a blacksmith. Soon he was selling his own metal tools.

Blacksmithing was a tough, grimy job, but Sequoyah enjoyed the hard work.

Sequoyah followed an old Cherokee tradition of painting. This paint pot is from the 1500s or earlier.

In his free time, Sequoyah began drawing and painting. He taught himself how to mix his own paints and make his own paintbrushes. He had a gift for capturing the world around him in his art.

In about 1809, Sequoyah found a new challenge. One day, he had an argument with some friends about talking leaves—written words. Sequoyah knew that some Cherokee people learned other languages. But he did not want to learn the languages of white people. He said that the Cherokee people could invent their own talking leaves. Then they could read and write in their own language.

Sequoyah's friends laughed at his idea. As a Cherokee leader once said, "My tongue is my pen and my mouth my paper." Native Americans used their memories and their mouths to pass down stories and send messages.

It had always been this way, his friends said. It wasn't right to meddle with this natural balance of things.

To many of Sequoyah's friends, writing seemed like a mysterious kind of magic that only white people were meant to have. Sequoyah disagreed. "The white man is no magician," he insisted.

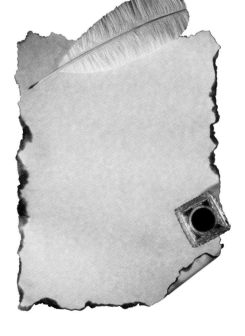

Sequoyah believed that Native Americans should be able to read and write in their own languages.

Sequoyah was sure he could find a way to write down Cherokee words. It would be a good challenge. And it would be good for Cherokee people. They could write down their own history in their own language. They could send written messages to each other.

A CHEROKEE LEGEND

A Cherokee storyteller once told Sequoyah a legend. The storyteller said the Great Spirit of all life had given white people and Native Americans two different gifts. The Great Spirit gave white people a bow and arrow. The Spirit gave Native Americans a book with writing in it, but they did not use it and soon forgot about it. One night, a white man stole the book and replaced it with the bow and arrow. The story meant that Native Americans should not use talking leaves, the storyteller said. But Sequoyah disagreed. He wanted to return the gift of writing to his people.

General Andrew Jackson

In 1813, an American general named Andrew Jackson came to the Cherokee people for help. He asked Cherokee men to join him in a war against Creek Indians. The Creeks lived on land that white farmers and settlers wanted. The Creeks had begun to fight for their homes.

The Cherokee didn't know if they could trust General Jackson. Americans had taken Cherokee land in the past. They had broken promises to the Cherokee people. Still, Cherokee leaders decided it was safest to side with the Americans against the Creeks. Otherwise, the Americans might fight the Cherokee people too.

Sequoyah joined the Creek War that fall. During the war, he noticed that many white soldiers used talking leaves. They sent letters to their families. People who read a soldier's letter would know his thoughts. They could learn news of the war from him. The Cherokee people deserved to have talking leaves too, thought Sequoyah.

Sequoyah returned home in the spring of 1814. With the fighting power of the Cherokee volunteers, Jackson had won the war against the Creeks.

The Creek War ended when the Creek chief Red Eagle (RIGHT) surrendered to Jackson (LEFT).

The Cherokee people had been a great help to the American soldiers. Sequoyah and his people hoped that the Americans would not forget the favor.

In 1815, Sequoyah married a Cherokee woman named Sally. The two of them set up a home and had children. Sequoyah had to work hard to take care of his new family. But he had not forgotten his promise to himself. He still wanted to solve the mystery of talking leaves.

3 MEETING THE CHALLENGE

In the fall of 1816, Andrew Jackson came to the Cherokee people once again. Sequoyah joined fourteen other Cherokee leaders in a meeting with the American general.

The meeting did not go well for the Cherokee leaders. Jackson wanted the men to sign an agreement called a treaty. The treaty said that the Cherokee people would sell some of their land to the United States. At first, Sequoyah and the others refused to sign the treaty. But Jackson told them that the U.S. government would take their land no matter what. It was better to give it up peacefully and earn some money for it.

This political cartoon shows the Cherokee people being injured and abused by white settlers.

Sequoyah and the other men did not want to lose any more land. But they didn't want it to be stolen either. In the end, they signed the treaty. Any Cherokee family who lived on the sold land would have to pack up and find another home.

Sequoyah's family was one of many who had to move. He signed up to join hundreds of Cherokee journeying westward to the Arkansas Territory. The U.S. government had promised them land there.

It was hard for Sequoyah and his family to give up their home and farm. Sequoyah left cattle and horses behind. Sally had to give up a spinning wheel and a loom that

she used to make clothing. But the greatest sadness was leaving Tuskegee forever.

Sally spun yarn and wove her own cloth at home.

Sequoyah did not want white people to push him so far from his home. At the last minute, he changed his mind about heading to Arkansas. Instead, he and Sally moved to a nearby Cherokee village in present-day Alabama called Willstown.

THE EASTERN AND WESTERN CHEROKEE NATIONS

U.S. treaties forced many Cherokee families to leave their homes and move westward. New arrivals joined a group of Cherokee who had already lived in the Arkansas Territory for many years. Cherokee in Arkansas were known as the Western Cherokee. Those who remained in the eastern homeland were called the Eastern Cherokee. The communities thought of themselves as separate Cherokee Nations with separate leaders and governments. Eventually, most Cherokee people formed one Cherokee Nation in Oklahoma. But the Eastern Band of Cherokee still exists. That community lives mostly in North Carolina.

Together, Sequoyah and Sally began building a cabin, planting and tending crops, and caring for their growing family. All the time, Sequoyah still thought about how to capture the Cherokee language in writing.

Around this time, Sequoyah came down with a strange illness. For days, he could not leave his cabin. But Sequoyah's mind was as sharp as ever. He quickly tired of staring at the wall in front of him. He escaped the boredom by thinking and thinking about talking leaves.

Sequoyah looked at the world more carefully once he was well again. He saw a woman carrying a baby in her arms. He saw a man laughing with his friend. He saw a graceful deer leaping through the woods.

Sequoyah wanted to use writing to describe the beauty of a leaping deer.

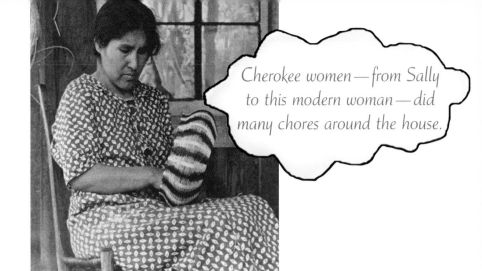

Cherokee women—from Sally to this modern woman—did many chores around the house.

The Cherokee language had words for all of these things. Sequoyah thought and thought about how he could make a drawing for each word.

Sequoyah's neighbors and family watched him make his strange drawings day after day. At first, they laughed at his work. But after a while, their laughter turned to alarm. Sequoyah had stopped caring for his crops. His farm was a mess of tall weeds and dry dirt. Sally complained that he never helped her with the chores.

People pleaded with Sequoyah to give up his foolish scribbling. Wasn't it dangerous to change the balance of life with these strange talking leaves?

Each time someone came to argue with him, Sequoyah listened politely. Then he pulled down his glasses, lit his pipe, and went right back to work.

One day, a friend told Sequoyah that the Cherokee people were worried he would make fools of them all. "You may tell them that what I am doing will not make fools of them," Sequoyah told his friend. "They did not cause me to begin, and they will not cause me to stop. . . . I shall go on, and you may tell our people." He understood his people's fear. But he did not share it. There was nothing foolish or dark about his talking leaves.

The small cabin where Sequoyah worked may have looked similar to this one.

Sequoyah believed he was close to creating a useful invention. But he needed more peace and quiet. He decided to build a small cabin away from his home.

Sequoyah spent hours at his little cabin, working on his drawings. His young daughter Ahyoka sometimes came to visit him, but nearly everyone else stayed away from him. They still hoped he would give up his mysterious work.

But Sequoyah's answer to the Cherokee people was clear. He was determined to keep working until he had invented a way to write down Cherokee words. Nothing would stop him.

4 SEQUOYAH'S INVENTION

The smell of thick smoke filled Sequoyah's cabin. Wild orange flames leapt out from the fireplace. Everything in the hearth burned to ashes. All of his work was gone.

Sequoyah did not lose faith in his idea, even when his work went up in flames.

Someone had set fire to Sequoyah's work. It could have been his wife or some frightened neighbors. But Sequoyah did not give up. He simply started over. He needed to think of a better idea anyway. Making a drawing for every word or idea was not practical. After all, who could remember so many drawings?

Sequoyah thought and thought until he came up with a new idea. He realized that every Cherokee word was made up of different sounds called syllables. He would capture each of these sounds with his ears the way a hunter captured a wild animal. Then he would make a drawing for each syllable.

Now when people spoke to him, Sequoyah hardly paid attention to what they said. Instead, he listened carefully for each sound they made. Over time, he discovered that about two hundred different sounds made up all the words in the Cherokee language.

Next came another challenge. Sequoyah had to create simple drawings for each sound. He did some more thinking. Then he remembered some of the letters that white people used for their words. He had learned to mark his jewelry with these letters. They seemed simple to draw and easy to remember. He decided to make his own simple letters for the Cherokee sounds.

People in different parts of the world have their own alphabets.

Sequoyah teaches the Cherokee alphabet to his daughter Ahyoka.

Two hundred letters were still too many to remember. With his daughter's help, Sequoyah narrowed the number of sounds down to eighty-six. Then he invented eighty-six letters that were easy to write, understand, and remember.

Sequoyah eagerly taught his new alphabet to Ahyoka. She learned it quickly. Soon the two of them could send each other messages and write down their conversations.

With great excitement, Sequoyah told his family and friends about what he had done. Most people did not believe him. Sequoyah was clever, they said. But he wasn't smart enough to make talking leaves.

Sequoyah's Alphabet

Each symbol of Sequoyah's alphabet stands for a different syllable sound. Putting the syllables together forms Cherokee words. For example, the word for "Cherokee" is *Tsa-la-gi*, or ᏣᎳᎩ. The word for "deer" is *a-wi*. Can you find the Cherokee symbols that make up this word?

Ꭰ a	Ꭱ e	Ꭲ i	Ꭳ o	Ꭴ u	Ꭵ i
Ꭶ ga Ꭷ ka	Ꭸ ge	Ꭹ gi	Ꭺ go	Ꭻ gu	Ꭼ gv
Ꭽ ha	Ꭾ he	Ꭿ hi	Ꮀ ho	Ꮁ hu	Ꮂ hv
Ꮃ la	Ꮄ le	Ꮅ li	Ꮆ lo	Ꮇ lu	Ꮈ lv
Ꮉ ma	Ꮊ me	Ꮋ mi	Ꮌ mo	Ꮍ mu	
Ꮎ na Ꮏ hna Ꮐ nah	Ꮑ ne	Ꮒ ni	Ꮓ no	Ꮔ nu	Ꮕ nv
Ꮖ qua	Ꮗ que	Ꮘ qui	Ꮙ quo	Ꮚ quu	Ꮛ quv
Ꮜ sa Ꮝ s	Ꮞ se	Ꮟ si	Ꮠ so	Ꮡ su	Ꮢ sv
Ꮣ da Ꮤ ta	Ꮥ de Ꮦ te	Ꮧ di Ꮨ ti	Ꮩ do	Ꮪ du	Ꮫ dv
Ꮬ dla Ꮭ tla	Ꮮ tle	Ꮯ tli	Ꮰ tlo	Ꮱ tlu	Ꮲ tlv
Ꮳ tsa	Ꮴ tse	Ꮵ tsi	Ꮶ tso	Ꮷ tsu	Ꮸ tsv
Ꮹ wa	Ꮺ we	Ꮻ wi	Ꮼ wo	Ꮽ wu	Ꮾ wv
Ꮿ ya	Ᏸ ye	Ᏹ yi	Ᏺ yo	Ᏻ yu	Ᏼ yv

Answer: ᎠᏫ

The people needed proof, Sequoyah thought. He decided to visit the Cherokee community that had settled in Arkansas. He taught his alphabet to a respected man there who was interested in Sequoyah's invention. Then Sequoyah asked the man to write a letter to a good friend in Willstown.

In the past, the man would have spoken his message out loud to a messenger. The messenger would memorize the message. Then he would travel to Willstown and repeat it to the man's friend. Sequoyah wanted to prove that his invention gave the Cherokee people an easier way to send messages long distances.

Sequoyah went home to Willstown with the letter. He read it in front of many Cherokee people. What they heard amazed them. The letter sounded exactly like messages that the man in Arkansas had sent in the past.

Sequoyah was delighted. He had done what he said he could do. He had given the Cherokee people the gift of talking leaves.

5 A TIME OF TEARS

Many Cherokee people still did not believe that Sequoyah's invention could work. He tested it again and again for them. Soon they stopped fearing the talking leaves. Sequoyah happily taught his people how to use the Cherokee alphabet for themselves.

Sequoyah's alphabet spread from neighbor to neighbor and friend to friend. Within a few months, hundreds of Cherokee people could read and write. People carved or painted letters on trees. They left messages on fences and homes. They used coal to write on bark or pieces of wood that they passed from one person to another.

In 1824, Sequoyah and his family decided to leave Willstown and join other Cherokee living in the Arkansas Territory. Sequoyah taught his Cherokee alphabet to as many people there as he could. A year later, the Cherokee honored him with a medal for the gift he had given to his people.

This famous portrait shows Sequoyah wearing his medal.

The CHEROKEE PHOENIX was the first newspaper printed in the Cherokee language.

Sequoyah's alphabet gave the Cherokee people a chance to do many new things. They stayed in touch more easily with written messages. They set up their own schools. In 1828, they began printing their own newspaper, the *Cherokee Phoenix*.

Some older Cherokee worried that their people were becoming too much like white people. But most Cherokee people believed that these changes made them stronger.

In 1829, Sequoyah and his family left home again. Andrew Jackson had been elected president. He wanted the Cherokee people to leave their land in Arkansas and move west to the Indian Territory in Oklahoma.

Many Cherokee people refused to leave their homes. But Sequoyah and Sally decided to go to Oklahoma. A new Cherokee Nation was forming there. Sequoyah could teach his alphabet to the people living in this community.

One year later, President Jackson put even more pressure on the Cherokee people and other Native Americans. In 1830, he signed the Indian Removal Act.

After leaving the Cherokee homeland, Sequoyah's family moved from Arkansas to the Indian Territory.

This law said that all Native Americans east of the Mississippi River had to leave their land and move west to Oklahoma. Jackson also convinced many Native Americans to sign treaties giving up their land.

Still, many Cherokee refused to move. In 1838, new president Martin Van Buren sent soldiers to all the Cherokee villages east of the Indian Territory in Oklahoma.

Martin Van Buren

The soldiers forced Cherokee families to leave their homes and most of their belongings behind. Then they made them travel thousands of miles across rivers and hills to Oklahoma. This sorrowful and difficult journey became known as the Trail of Tears.

TRAIL OF TEARS

The Trail of Tears was a terrible time in American history. It took place from 1838 to 1839. Cherokee men, women, and children were first taken from their homes and gathered in crowded, dirty prison camps. Deadly illnesses spread easily in these camps, and many people died. When fall came, the Cherokee were forced to march thousands of miles to the Indian Territory. They did not have proper food or clothing, and many more people died. In all, at least four thousand Cherokee people lost their lives during the Trail of Tears.

After a long, hard winter, homeless Cherokee families began to arrive in the Indian Territory. They were weary. Many of them were hungry or sick. They missed their old homes.

Sequoyah and Sally wanted to do all they could to welcome the Cherokee people after the Trail of Tears. But some leaders of the Cherokee Nation were not so welcoming.

Cherokee families marched thousands of miles on the Trail of Tears.

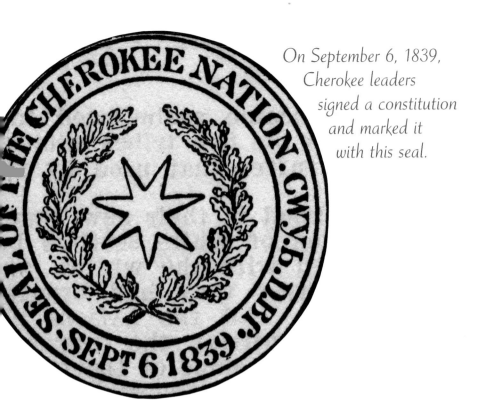

On September 6, 1839, Cherokee leaders signed a constitution and marked it with this seal.

They had worked hard to set up a Cherokee government in Oklahoma. Some of the newly arrived Cherokee leaders wanted to make changes. They had different ideas about how the government should work.

Sequoyah knew that the Cherokee Nation would fail if its different groups did not work together. He talked to the leaders of both sides and made peace between the two groups.

Now Sequoyah had a new challenge. He wanted to bring all of the Cherokee people together in peace. He knew that some Cherokee people lived in Texas. With his encouragement, many of them came to live on the Cherokee land in Oklahoma.

Sequoyah had also heard about a community of Cherokee people living in Mexico. But no one knew exactly where they were. Sequoyah decided to find the Cherokee people in Mexico.

This statue of Sequoyah holding his alphabet is carved from a giant redwood tree.

The trip to Mexico was a long one, and Sequoyah was getting to be an old man. He was not as strong as he had once been. On the way to Mexico, he became seriously ill. He died in the summer of 1843.

The Cherokee people were sad to lose such a good leader and friend. But they were grateful for the gift he had given them. They were grateful for his lively mind and his loyal heart. He had worked hard to keep the Cherokee people strong. And he never stopped believing in the power of talking leaves.

TIMELINE

In the year . . .

1790? Sequoyah became a silversmith.   Age 25

1809? he began thinking about the talking leaves.

1813   he fought in the Creek War on the side of the American troops.   Age 48

1815   he married Sally.

1816   he and fourteen other Cherokee leaders met with Andrew Jackson and signed a treaty giving up some of their land.   Age 51

1819? he and Sally moved to Willstown. he came down with a serious illness.

1820? his work was destroyed in a fire.

1821   he presented his alphabet to the Cherokee people.   Age 56

1824   he and his family moved to the Arkansas Territory.

1825   the Cherokee people presented him with a medal for his work.

1829   he and his family moved to the Indian Territory in Oklahoma.   Age 64

1830   President Andrew Jackson signed the Indian Removal Act.

1838   the Trail of Tears began as thousands of Cherokee families are forced to leave their homes and move westward.

1843   he died on his way to find the Cherokee people living in Mexico.   Age 78

Honoring Sequoyah

Many people have heard of the giant sequoia trees of California—the world's largest trees. But did you know that these mighty redwoods were named after Sequoyah? They are just one way that people have honored and remembered the Cherokee inventor. Here are some others:

• The Sequoyah Statue in Washington, D.C., is in the Hall of Statues in the nation's Capitol. The hall contains one statue from each state. In 1917, Oklahomans chose a statue of Sequoyah to represent their state.

• The Sequoyah Birthplace Museum is located in Vonore, Tennessee. It honors Sequoyah and the Cherokee people.

• Sequoyah High School in Tahlequah, Oklahoma, is run by the Cherokee Nation.

• The Sequoyah Book Award has been given each year since 1859. Children and young adults in Oklahoma choose their favorite book for this award in memory of Sequoyah and his gift of the written Cherokee language.

• Sequoyah County is located in eastern Oklahoma where the state borders Arkansas.

FURTHER READING

NONFICTION

Bruchac, Joseph. *The Trail of Tears.* **New York: Random House, 1999.** This illustrated book is about the Cherokee removal and the Trail of Tears.

Flanagan, Alice K. *Mrs. Scott's Beautiful Art.* **New York. Children's Press, 1999.** This book describes the work of a Cherokee artist who uses many natural materials to create art in the tradition of her Cherokee ancestors.

Lowery, Linda. *Wilma Mankiller.* **Minneapolis: Carolrhoda Books, Inc. 1996.** This biography tells the life story of the Cherokee people's first female leader.

Roop, Peter and Connie Roop. *If You Lived with the Cherokee.* **New York: Scholastic, 1998.** This book describes what life was like for Cherokee children and adults long ago.

Santella, Andrew. *The Cherokee.* **New York: Children's Press, 2001.** Learn about Cherokee food, homes, clothing, and customs in this book.

FICTION

Pennington, Daniel. *Itse Selu: Cherokee Harvest Festival.* **Watertown, MA: Charlesbridge, 1994.** This book follows Cherokee boy Little Wolf as he enjoys a traditional Cherokee celebration. A note about Sequoyah and his alphabet is in the back of the book.

Roop, Peter, and Connie Roop. *Ahyoka and the Talking Leaves.* **New York: Lothrop, Lee and Shepard Books, 1992.** This novel imagines how Sequoyah's daughter Ahyoka might have helped her father create his alphabet.

WEBSITES

Official Site of the Cherokee Nation
<http://www.cherokee.org> This website has information about Sequoyah, the Cherokee language, and Cherokee history and culture. The site also has a special kids' section.

Tsalagi Language Resources
<http://public.csusm.edu/raven/cherokee.dir/cher1.html> Check out this website for a small Cherokee glossary and for information about Sequoyah's alphabet.

SELECT BIBLIOGRAPHY

Foreman, Grant. *Sequoyah.* Norman, OK: University of Oklahoma Press, 1938.

Hoig, Stan. *The Cherokees and Their Chiefs: In the Wake of Empire.* Fayetteville, AR: The University of Arkansas Press, 1998.

Hoig, Stan. *Sequoyah: The Cherokee Genius.* Oklahoma City: Oklahoma Historical Society, 1995.

Payne, John Howard. "Notable Persons in Cherokee History: Sequoyah or George Gist." *Journal of Cherokee Studies,* Fall 1977, 385–393.

Perdue, Theda, ed. *Cherokee Editor: The Writings of Elias Boudinot.* Athens, GA: The University of Georgia Press, 1996.

Wallace, Anthony F. C. *The Long Bitter Trail: Andrew Jackson and the Indians.* New York: Hill and Wang, 1993.

INDEX

Acknowledgments

For photographs and artwork:
© Courtesy of The Atlanta History Center, front cover, p. 35; © From a painting by Carlyle Urello. Courtesty, Tennessee State Museum, p. 4; © Tennessee State Museum Collection, pp. 8, 36; © Photowood Inc./CORBIS, p. 9; Smithsonian Institution National Anthropological Archives, Bureau of American Ethnology Collection, p. 11; © North Wind Picture Archives, pp. 13, 17, back cover; © Thomas E. Mails, Cherokee People published 1992 by Council Oak Books, p. 14; © Tecmap Corporation; Eric Curry/CORBIS, p. 15; Library of Congress, pp. 18, 30 (right); © Bettmann/CORBIS, pp. 21, 41; © Danny Lehman/CORBIS, p. 22; © Chase Swift/CORBIS, p. 24; © CORBIS, pp. 25, 42; © Oconaluftee Indian Village, p. 26; © Paul A. Souders/CORBIS, p. 29; Korean Overseas Information Service, p. 30 (left); Western History Collections, University of Oklahoma Library, p. 31; Library of Congress, LC-USZ62-1738, p. 38; Collection of the State Museum of History, Oklahoma Historical Society, p. 40; Library of Congress, LC-USZ62-3764, p. 45.
For quoted material: p. 15, 26, Hoig, Stan. Sequoyah: The Cherokee Genius. Oklahoma City: Oklahoma Historical Society, 1995; p. 15, Payne, John Howard. "Notable Persons in Cherokee History: Sequoyah or George Gist." *Journal of Cherokee Studies* (Fall, 1977): 385-393.